MW01612381

evaporatus

Poems By
Christopher Klingbeil

Winner, 2013 of The Jenny Catlin Chapbook Competition, Jenny Catlin, Judge

ELJ Publications, LLC
ELJ Editions Series

ISBN: 1-942004-01-1
ISBN-13: 9781-942004-01-1

for Courtney

CONTENTS

ACKNOWLEDGMENTS

Several poems in this collection have been published in the following journals in various forms: *Utter* and *Vinyl Poetry*.

a night in temporal portmanteaux

may this record of mechanical failure be the dreaming place I'd like to
not quite name. where the flux afforded in an opening invitation is
discarded envelopes and poor cartoons. where the stop-motion verbs:
we're in: wherein: a portmanteaux peals back in the ringing of cathedral
bells

for sunday in a smog and to start if you see the calendar open. insert
directives for a film crew here: in the panorama which you built for
school what color is the church stone? and how empty are the streets?
just how many bulletins thrown to wind by children in a fit for a
warmer spring begin to look like birds at sea? and how long has it been
raining? until now. yes.

which would be your method against crabbing up along the riverways
as you moved? sculling past stone bridges, hillside hotels, the coastal
rails and wooden stairs over empty streets in the lower districts of a
populace of pastels. through the soil underneath, remember. an oil
painting for how to say let's see lake baikal or its character in ancient
chinese. so many underscores for how the fluid representational
conundrum truly is

in these lacustrine cities. the set support may carry on in sharp and
intermittent waves. as attending to. and tending to leave relief. so just
what was I intending? and who were you? the opening letter of us
together always mending we

we left for the brink of the pier at dawn. and we traveled for so
long. we were the documentaries for futuristic armed forces
parades. flying ships with photon lasers and the like. we carried
on by settling the coast and enduring winter. not jumping at the
heavy boom of breaking ice as each spring breaks again defiant. I
came to set paper boats to sail against the world's oldest lake and
you attended to the water with a diligence for cultivation. for the
media for crossing its breadth. attaining canvas then coal. water
cycles toward fusion in the shaking cold

yet still. you might emerge yet still from a riverside tunnel at the
locks. your hands each free to amend the five foot cranes skating
on thin ice. white on slate on stilts across the melting snow. the
woods on either side a wilted architecture for how some long-
forgotten pier you've never been to see is this thatching for a
record of mechanical failure. where we run the risk announcing
verb as noun. you're not in russia after all

might that be enough to avoid an overlap of the water and those
shapes we've named by their reflection's continuity across the
atmosphere / o, might my image overlap and echo in the
bleating water wake

blood orange woods

I've started walking through the blood orange woods. that is, the sky is low and gray. having just rained. maybe raining still. many movements in between the trees possessive of a gothic anomaly: continuous motion verb. verb at rest in a process of continuance from the clouds above. as a conditional. raining still. no. I've confused the noun of this graph already

it wasn't an orange grove but the oaks drenched with leaves in the rain that left the woods blood orange. if I listen to their tapping made by dropping rain on leaves. and you fill your stomach's groan with a charcoal sketch of naked trees. we might draw in. where together. is the term for any given perspective of the tempo water takes to leave the pond when raining as raining is a crater of the fluid surface. to characterize the mood now moving through the trees. ask when breathed and naming under water will answer the question to your name for us

room for salvation

pretty sure it was you. who was asking if there was a room for
salvation when I started thinking about that cabin we'd visited so
hopelessly out in the woods when we were young? it didn't look
like much from outside. standing there years later in the snow
and filled with the type of dull ache I suspect lingers in the
layered paint of famous landscape oils. even a perimeter of
artificial puddles couldn't discredit the ochre flares sent up by
grass unraveling from the snow. we talked until it seemed a
wonder that not one of the almanacs we carried wasn't simply
ten thousand photos taken of this one place. at rates reaching
greater than one photo for each day's hour of a year. but we had
yet to enter the cabin. we hadn't really grasped the physical
notion of hauling all that weight. tomes of a flip book landscape
enough to fill the mausoleum. whereas a book of empty records
became a type of monument we'd carried throughout the
pouring weather to place inside the cabin. to mark it as an empty
tomb. I think lost in translation is an ever-present term. the way
the room of records made the room for hanging sketches an
evolution for blank canvas followed by concentric layers of wet
paint. we entered. twirling through open space of the room we
afforded the record its landscape entered in

necessitated image

that is to say the image necessitated of itself as you might imagine
meiosis to understand the meaning of yourself. name a device for
perpetuating a recurrence of yourself. name the noun the series holds
captive in a smog of missing parts. how might the story unfold.
precisely. imperceptibly. most times the story holes up as a narrative of
a place you can't remember if you've been to. I've heard the purpose of
rearranging drawers in a dream is for reducing clerical error.
classification continuity for later on. yet I've yet to wake to the name as
it's changed. therein, as much. a certain family of stellar jays still follows
us along the pines. tinge of blue still in the faintest imagining of birds
in the needles whenever we get the chance to move

room of its own

the inside cabin walls are green with rust and the wooden barber chair in a room of its own sits empty in the sun. in the room of one's own there is a minimum of one name. from there, as in many a house of records, meiosis most appears through hanging string from name to name

two dreams

at two laments of two perfect dreams I'm in the sea or in a tunnel in the sea underneath the water and in a texttype I called wetland jungle for how the serifs hang about in paintings of raphael. stale blue air and the slate of herons in the trees.

in another I'm investigating a box of records of myself and find I have two names. or the office has confused my records with someone else entirely. each permutations of the bodies I'd never been. or again. and once again. for so many times the form has yet to be as the crossroads in the woods becomes dependent upon what you've read. or if you'd been both the roads. and the traveler for whom I never could have been

in a cut of woods between the streams. beside the river where I remember another river. one heron floats in the blue between the water and the dammed and the reflection of itself inside the water

dates

the record of the process rests in frames you've chosen to call by number. perhaps I was so terribly incredible at being so terrible at talking to you on the phone that I took revenge on the dialpads of tax-free calculators. I moved to a state that shape of your phone number and I stole from its department stores a hollow insatiable pleasure. equating with a number among the pages which rest between so many settled layers. all the stories we've never settled to store between us. pluck a rubber number from the pad and speak to it. we might have been geologists together is what I said. about the double plot still left. if you remember. wide open to ourselves

this saying to myself

this saying to myself. I cannot see in the weight of daylight so delicate
a rise as lining for a life unless I turn away. unless this scrawling
through the heft. the rise and sky the page cast out as letters in the
clouds and gathering toward dismissal. fainted orphans in the absence
spaces of blue vessels. pillar in the skin a pallor in the clouds. of light
a vessel carried left-text sheen. recollection strata. fallen page to limp
and travel in rivulets through the printed test a light runs through. as
if beneath the agency of the clouded sky my eyes could comprehend
the pressure taken in the space the words might fill

athenaeum

eventually the reproductive rate of windows turning to mirrors
replicates. everyone's story about how they came to the book of
records ends with a cabin in the canyon box. beside the river.
I've named every imaginable chameleon that's flotsam'ed by.
been stung any number of times. founded an athenaeum in the
memory of myself and looked to each appropriate article within
it when pronunciation resembled the movements of myself.
names of family trees escaped as the weather pressed on
through. or, eventually: all I have to write on is the memory of
myself where occasionally you enter. holding papers for the
name

eremites

if you address any of your names to the affixed constellations and wave the anchor to the world may seem to wobble while passing on. according to the moon the ingenuity of seasons falling directly into one another is where the geologist party cast about in groves along the dust until they found their ancients' home by air. does everything the eremitic does become serendipitous? or does it merely does? so much time has passed inside the grammar it's getting hard to tell. the fourth wall to the wall of records did not require participation from the previously hidden whereas the waves have been doing their thing for just a while. salt was added so much later in the crinkle of leaves beside the river

slough

just so happened we happened upon the record in a cabin on an
unadorned night. the slough outside consumed the starlight so
the stench of mycology drew a delicate path through the cypress'
toppling leaves. in a mold made braced for the toppling toward
the eventual pool yet another leaf leapt through soil. stumps of
desiccated grass made stoops for tripping through. wobbled
skipping in pathology. we drifted off to dead tissue. slough
severed from the tissue surrounding or what the snake effused.
everyone's feet so wet and cold trouncing through the dark.
tonguing distant memories by scent to see by fire. we arrived at
the steps of the record shed where we went off along our
separate ways according to which ways the wood grain took our
breath.

in the dark the record was waking to the humid swamp. a host of
human bodies crawling on the paneled walls in sandpaper skin
and soughing breath into each woodgrain's gap. drawing by
breath the smallest length of indecipherable words. words the
record homes in sonar. lips along the clapboards' recorded
weather.

to navigate the smallest extent of a lips' passing rouge and
whether the shadow in my palm or fingerprints yields a breadth
consumed in entering in. the record desk found nameless in a
book of records filled with namelessness. faces in the wall
around the field with mirrors in my mouth

warehouse

rough-hewn in a disassembled scent you might populate a warehouse by yourself. mown across last century's dust in collections along the shelf. a team of light and stone and their eradication into an opposition of themselves. water arranged by phenotype along the shelves casts a spectrum of fading light for the party streamers to loop through. through the light we found our lines. perhaps in the other room, away from the windows. they spoke of the others. searing away the rust by lathe. we left a corrugated text in the preserves

the red cross

the red cross deployed an ambulatory bank capable of holding only one person's money at a time.

I've been destroying hindsight by extending public forums to excruciating lengths by mentioning that most fashionably late debates have yet to literally end.

whereas the artwork's hanging watercolor scheme interrogated you by hustling filibusters through museum halls. demanding dates for the forums by which to define the light. slow enough to skew the light. the paintings turned a type of blood on blank. you'll try to tape this from my view. yet each has pled the passing fifth.

while the tree leaves grew throughout the water spilling down the page. erased azure through the river's color gave the wall a suggestion that cannot remember where it ends or if this will be the final installment before the occupation ends

bloodroot hearts in an impressionist torrent set swirling threw the page. I'd play the film of coursing through the color wheel at varying speeds for unsuspecting patrons. rolling eyes and crossing teeth by the time they hear the nurses have taken, still to this day as digital extras, to staying in their practiced calm. *The veins of light you see breaking lighted space around is how you see we've all confected.*

so the auroras lit. our film ended with silent era dancing. outside, an impregnable ribbon of blood abounds again in the space between constellations. her blue linen cuffs on the nurse's blouse as real and false as the party streamers pointed to

convalesced

convalesced on the porch where the golden light pooled deepest until rustled up by a flock of orange. leaves in the wind took a trip out past the tracks to see a thousand geese spell vortex in the sun-bleached blue. in concert is my favorite prepositional

image a day

an image a day keeps the graveyard away. unless you're thinking of dates. I've been attempting to collect the same picture I took by painting a suitcase of that photo in a thousand prints. paints and fingers for a frozen lake. ashore acrylics in the aether. the waxy diorama of vegetation in the light suggested. I mean to move through a spectrum. each print succession for a tone of blue. each almanac the measure for how I'd arrive in these steps along the wall. where the times new roman tattoo gallery ran a line of increasingly smaller text around the room and where the paragraph gave way

long-standing history

I have a long-standing history of being interrupted on the final page of every story ever read. while difficult to prove, I suspect this correlates with the number of hours I've spent getting wasted on a few dollars in government warehouses. there's usually a lot of dust on the fat brown clock who shelves from an industrial grade school. just about everything's lacking graffiti. mostly pencils suggest the way for the wall of orphan screws and nails and bolts to washer ever slowly off. so send this curious circumference off to ha. I had a dream on the way back to work where I'd see this river in the window from my truck from sixty years away. we might be one hundred and one percent unchanged. & yet we might be all the canyons ever visited. I can't tell if we teach a complex lesson on the natures of dust while the always yellowed lignin returns eventually to my attention. by the time a paragraph's returned to my attention. has worn away. or if I've just now made the page that way

panopticon

spatially, I grew curious, extending the cabin walls in circumference around established decking to form the geometric horizon where dust might grow. did I say it was a film which looped across the cabin walls, or a well? which was always partially true. the globe held a dome with the dyes of every shade of every lifestage of a rosebulb to light each room each day with the appropriate season. while the center of the room was behind me.

which explains the focusing perspective I had in installing a panopticon to wheel throughout the room as the party guest I'd only invited over with expectations for it not to come.

but of course it does and we spend the night craftily eluding visibility of one another. which isn't to say the shapes of our shadows throughout the room aren't inherently interesting. but I'd rather have stayed home until I invented the carousel and took to recording the shapes it made in passing on the walls. at first by the easiest of discernible names. the usual horses by which we'd grow hobbled by the losses of overhead light. the eventual charcoal twisting shapes of the names toward the messy pool at shadow's edge

dance party

funny part about the cave is the symphony sounds drastically different
to the varying number of spelunkers as they descend on the grand
piano's difference of string. this tends to compromise the identification
of shadows when spun along the wall. usually tinsel is the leading
misnomer in periphery. spiderwebs may be held in high regard as the
performance drags along but it seems the elderly appreciate having
geometry most of all raised on archaic penal codes. too often the
populace imagines the cave as having one way in and one way out.
come midnight, many on the floor complain of dancing to the same
songs as they've heard before they realized they knew they'd been here
for this long. so-so gyrations continued. worked out wondrous ways
for chains to make an orchestra for the ways our fingers tremble

platonic condition

the platonic condition defined a romantic absence in the heart of the imprisoned point of view. the heart of the cave. that is, when proper noun was possessed of a theoretical love. verbs like trampolines in imagination, or in jumping across. perhaps the softest meaning of light tonguing at the bloodpump in the ears. can you hear the firelight without looking up? for the longest time dolomites caught stars by evacuating embers. drew the night along the walls by soot. all along the faintest film of charcoal we found the night unveiling. many of the walls drew closer. as the ceiling lowered slowly. closed-mouth teeth of the cave became the weight of bones we'd left by those above

onion ring

funny thing about the cabin is that it wasn't really real unless you
thought about it. or if you'd take us to the woods to paint the fallen
needles in the pines remembrance. the way the driveway was more
visible in the dark. clearing of legs to the contour of an entrance. we
didn't have to look up at the missing stars to know it might snow in
any second. beside the river we'd developed a particular gift for
knowing weather by its waterscent. light was another matter. orion
appeared in a spackle of flakes thrown in storm on the morning
horizon, and in the layering of light and sunlight the constellation
seemed a sight of permanent seizure

honey

which conflated hero had I cast myself? depended on the night
dependent on the wall I'd painted bright enough to catch and
release by even the lightest film. called the constellations and
made popcorn every night until no one answered. most of our
relationship began to make sense in platonic caves. most
shadows spun into a hustled walk through crowded streets and
something of the way the daylight lit the skyline gold reminded
me of the canyon where we'd waded through the river where so
many tenants in hive had never yet conceived to visualize.
occupied a collective suggestion of yourself nonetheless. as
honeycombs spread out on sandstone. I was here to tell the city
of great wonders in the west while through no fault of their own,
you've already been. so, well. when the cave is also in a vortex
there's probably another cave around. see, you could trace the
shadows spiraling up and down the stairs into a calendar of days
and follow this constellation of shoulders and crowns to find a
third horizon between the sky and ground

out to pasture

eventually your favorite band plays a country song and you know it's
over. if you've been listening to the country this entire while perhaps a
sudden realization of the spectral band's potential may irrevocably
release you from the wrap of prickly cricket fingers. though this is rare.
painting purple flowers in the wheat beside your love is painting the
very same scene is reimagining taking the scene away. one might blink
yet one might blink and yet one might blink and yet one might restore
the polaroid factory to prominence. once again. or if you take a course.
to say nothing of the paint you remember in periphery. rest of the
scene still wet on the palette left

a peeling

most mornings opened as a peeling. I didn't know for some time the reeds didn't contain a nest of wind-up toys creaking in the spring. the most epauletted blackbirds were in large part mostly responsible for every legislative horoscope contained within the job description. each day an almanac opened to the color of yesterday's color slightly hidden, and the task was to ask which shade of the morning's fog was out of focus. which would stay as snow. which would stay the snow by forecasting inverted weather. which rate of smoke might translate a frequency to form a noun evaporate. as a distillate. as any break in the clouds to prove the marsh was broken. yellowed teeth too soft to whistle. black birds with red shoulders pleading for their kin to hatch from bells before they sing

whether

you know it's always been about you. but with me. think of the weather in as many positions as you can. every minutia of precipitation seen distilled in separate scenes across the wall. become a randomness for which tornados are no more spectacular. a perception. echo of the self as an exception in the person. don't expect the plot to drive a rectangle. or a story to distract from horrific ice spells. or a reason to obey the natural call for moving underground

escape routes

escape routes became more difficult as the plans were named. calling the cave our cabin, for instance, served quite nicely as a setting out to sea. as you might imagine, wielding axes from the forest in the rolling waves became the awkward seizure of our time. I started claiming the evaporative properties of soil by calling your name again and again. the lining of my mouth metallic with a humus which suggested against betting on the success of my pride. the shores approached us. already? I hadn't even yet had cabin fever. which was always the great worry. how might an echo of our passage fall to weight the land? there were a thousand incantations in the rain as we cast about

the northmost post

several devout few sequestered their record deep inside the northmost post. it was all they had to read. larch trees stood out most against the color of themselves in other trees. food grew scarce too often. eventual pilgrimage was made of the northmost post, planting rye in well-spaced lines along the way to mark the way and those paths back. most trying were those dazed by fasting through their resources. to dwell for so long beside the river put confetti in the ears of many and many expeditions from established record simply failed to return. the most well-fed of drones for falling stars to confirm advancements in technology cast a slow parade

comedy_break

thin out a morse code message for recorded history. concentrate the breadth of time by coloring paper. color like makes one want to say ochre. like where we wore a lot of ochre in our walks beside the river. where hemingway wrote the world's greatest telegrams. we filled tall colors in wooden barns. painted in the leafless wood. advanced to collections of electronic pulse attached to paper and the paper fused. to ward away any sense of tattered edges.

we walked until we couldn't choose which messages went where. lost control of the whole blending of placing edges. as puzzle pieces in that autumn's almanac read aloud our tailored measurements to ourselves until the repetition of ourselves faded from blurring out our vision. we walked around in public saying stop. the cops started issuing tickets for not stopping full.

but as if ambivalence for the ambivalent message of a recorded failure device should scare us back to working order. stripping paint from fashionable broadsides went on to write perfect wikipedia pages for nick adams. who gained notoriety enough to go off and be the rake young ladies whispered about around corral corners? secretly admiring love stories shared with the advancing news mustaches had grown back in style. truly everyone thought we were getting @therealrebel_jonny_yuma when a handsome fabrication rolled into town. together we checked our phones until it meant something more than the fetters of shredded paper still fuming at his pearly boots

cave painting

most times I get to thinking the cabin was just some place I paid rent
to place myself inside the series of stories it took to understand the
cabin's single story. the landlords let me paint the walls. public
television spat wet smoke dramatizations across my outstretched hands
and the clay helped to score my place inside the cave. so much for
reading in the reds and ochre of the light against the alley brick outside.
for eventually the news formed paper in the river ice by stones lain
gently at first to note the way through snow. resulting pools of imprint
announced the contour of the path we'd taken between the fingerprints
of everything we'd neglected to pick up. an article of clothing for the
naked ground we grew commonplace until lost in the weight of
themselves

canary colony

none of which is to say I've spoken a word of the canary colony
to anyone. instead, I've used my credentials to gain access to the
city which passes with a comet through the night at such a speed
the buildings in the city each shine gold. twentynine stories
underground the warehouse walls of the city's intestine throb
with a crayola yellow and all the PA speakers effuse chalky bird
dust. sunflower seeds and icy breath, the bones of the forest in a
plaza of the city we'd been trained to forget had been its capitol.
we breathed the dust enough to be transfixed and then stood
around in our sleepwear, waiting in purgatorial lines for more
channels to comatose to. once I got so happy I couldn't smile
any harder. I was the only one in the restless club while the
constant heather glare of the place sold a lot of umbrellas. some
of the older patients adapted a beach club named the sungrazers
while I'd been conspiring to break free. building capacity to pass
through warehouse layers without being gassed. sliding past
elevator guards in the melting gravity like dropping from the
high dive. holding my air. by the time I reached the surface I was
so lightheaded I began to name the constellations whirling
throughout the comet's golden turrets and capitol buildings. the
gutted linen shops and bank lights falling over darkened alleys
and recently broken glass reflecting back to space the image of
itself I can't remember if I couldn't breathe or not. it wasn't that
I couldn't not recall whose bones I'd breathed in the speakers'
dust, but that the nomenclature for any comet is both the first
and last in its fate of events. I had been forced to breathe the
names in the dust and that had been reason enough for escape.
and the outside lights above the city were just so very clean

whether weather

should the frequency of participation effect how we bare the scene. I'm going to make millions by the turn of the sun selling tall drinks in the open plaza with enough patio space to accommodate the entire daylight. open the doors that will remain unlocked during daylight hours. shepherd clientele slowly through the show in half arc circles. seats nearest the epicenter will sell out quick yet I suspect so much from the corner windows. the recursive tear in a nightlife's fabric opens with this day and ends by softly stitching together its skin. again to the empty tables in the farthest turns of the sun. collecting rust in shades faster than we can re-stock the placemat crayons for painting landscapes with

dear future

getting the feeling camp is just a game of getting as many items into the smallest plastic I can carry. I'm O+ if you need my platelet number. or if you want to know just how many clinking drinks under starlight become the same eventual pair of dad shorts in a fold-out chair. I'll run an ice pick across the poles to confirm the romantic future tense if you'll remember the meadow where the woods' roofline in the passing rain became a palette for the clearing sky. one day we'll still be an ice click away from where the glaciers stood me up. everyday the volcano is someone we've always heard about in another language and have made many attempts to sabotage. the native tongue that is. while I've been used as an adjunct toward healing for several decades the crossword for which tone-atone event is amino acids precludes just where we've been. as in this now empty crater never yielded so many blank answers to the question

denominator

where there must be is a denominator found in the commonality
between the reader of record and record is the wave light intercepts to
provide a sound for time having passed through. this is also called the
atmosphere. and passing through. the winding in your breath lets me
know I'm in serious trouble I may yet be resolved of. as any break in
the spring yields the flatness of summer. close the record yet endure
the echo. while the reason for cicadas still is

em dash battled

this story begins with the battle scenes drawn-up in middle
school. it only takes a few lines to form horizon and perspective.
cluster bomb the landscape with a stick broken into minutemen.
the duration of any battle is devised of any number of sticks
risen up through thin air and disposed of with ink. ballistics
becomes the study of dotted lines between your memory of the
scene before the men and this littered page of red. sound effects
are much encouraged. there's always something so very simple in
every single story you've ever heard. and yet I forget. whoever
settled the score between our ballpoint pens? remember how the
bows and arrows made of mutilated plastic with rubber bands
became a toy for every compliment we'd not yet learned to send?
a continent is this space between my yet and then

time machine

I've been wasting my turn with the time machine to correct old jokes that didn't fly. after we revisited the conquistadors and you persuaded me to forget about running with the bulls the methods for self-improvement became rather cyclical. mainly I wanted to remember myself as having accomplished a better version of myself. not saying anything except except kept me intact the longest. instead began to softly color in the almanac with acrylic depictions of the fauna. each pic a floral petal for the past apartments I've shared with people in a text oblivious to your existence. and yes. soon enough there will be another photo of our house to patch across this paragraph

ecology dictates

mainly I've been meaning to tell you how. the drape of passing clouds across the plains evokes a sense of dashing lines along a discursive page. there must be something relative of remembering the scent lead leaves smirked against the page. paper an autumn milkweed. crisp dough on the weight of colored rice. returned to husk to fatten out unto. the prairie's grass soon desiccated by domestic teeth. a breath forewarning precipitous events which yet unspoken prepare the swirl of this body. so quaint to know that the prairie has two i's. while if I'm not always so scared of dying in the margin I might yet still provide the swill for crawling through. to land from sea yet once again. but then again. it's not my fault not everyone comprehends ecology

fretted clay

too much of this projection has begun with obsessions over ribs and breadth. as hendiadys for a cage becomes at root with homonyms for how. I'm no better than a dictionary for how we've twisted out of context. which is to say my vital organs have wished to equate with the contest between air and light. so I've divested a few too many. does it matter if the photosynthetic process is still on track? if this body is akin to clay pots I've placed around my palms and my plants' lives and the metaphor isn't about anything remotely beautiful cliché. rather how the ghosts of my skin and my family's skin have woven inside-out across the flowering stage and continued throughout the roses lofted through the globe. latinate leaves along the trellis and the frame through which the light is named

agency/device

window panes from before your century bauble in the warp the view has taken in. distortion is a ghost walk I've taken along the streets where all my friends have moved. how many reproductions of yourself will have entered through a glaring mirror to find you are still yet so far away? the daylight setting north erased azure and in the avalanche slim shifts of marigold. clouds deceptive as mountains. accumulating slowly. as the word for snow from before we'd known the weather or how the wind might blanket us. the portmanteaux I've spoken of, I should mention, was misnomer for how the agency became device. the record was begotten. and in the lineage rests a folded canvas. paint along the ribs exposed by the deepest exhumation

strikethat

strikethat. the name of my village when all I wanted when I grew up
was to be the king of a village we'd soon antiquary. but we never spoke
like that when we were kids until we found our tongues. to this day I
can summon the entire script of the tape we cast. squiggling a
basement away. my favorite bands played a percussion rasp along the
river's handle and I can't get past the way there's still hope for the type
writer. just about every great narrative I've invented begins with an
impossibly probable scenario of assuming positions in the great
economy for twisting language into rope

the evaporatus

eventualized construction of the evaporatus by thinking astronomically. procured a record amount of support from independent donors to erect a series of enormous wedding bands around the stratosphere. had sun tea on the porch where we became our favorite time for spreading gossip on the weather. at certain lights the atmosphere looked like glass inside the silver spines and I set out and drew the light. lowered shades for the negative spaces left by trees and waited for the stars to shape a necessary blush for when the glass had worn away

fortune cookie

in the fortune cookie business model there are any number of
casualties. the old joke is blaming fate for the next lesson of skewered
letters in a copy jam of intentioned lectures

author photo

I was dreaming of my author photo forecasted in the sun when tickets to yuma fell from the ordinary sun. why is it that the desert compels me to take inordinate pictures of myself? I've been walking through the charcoal woods with the sky so high and bright and with the ordinary sunlight I'd forgotten you looked up. the needlelessness the fire left leaves a smoky line along our chin. requesting please be me my impersonation. myself is not quite me. or move beside myself in a wake and see what moves between

tandem

somebody still loves that fatty nub above the elbows as coupling is no
mistake when you find the right vortex. there's so much unflattering
dna along this city's streets I can't seem to keep my feet from getting
the dry cleaning. beauty was such a fickle note we'd sung until we
found the wear of myself throughout deserted streets. in portraiture
online and where there's versions of myself I've never been. apologies.
by my versions of your shoulders in the moon I've known you through
so many versions of yourself you've never seen. remember how we'd
joked of boating and then began? it was a little like that. except for the
rain and wind

ABOUT THE AUTHOR

Christopher Klingbeil has toured the American West as a government lumberjack and forester. He took MFAs away from Boise State University and Colorado State University. Once, he took an Honorable Mention in *The Atlantic's* Student Writing Contest. His poems and stories have appeared in *Salt Hill*, *Smoking Glue Gun*, *Vinyl Poetry*, and elsewhere.